THE GOLFER'S SURVIVAL GUIDE

About the Author

Charles Rapshot comes from a long line of Rapshots: Cecile Rapshot and Cedric Rapshot, going back to the first person in their family to ever play the game. No one remembers his full name, but on the course, he was known to players, caddies and anyone who'd seen him play as 'Mr C.Rapshot'.

THE GOLFER'S SURVIVAL GUIDE

Excuses, Tips, Tricks and
Ways to Finally Enjoy Your Game

CHARLES RAPSHOT

WELBECK

Copyright © Charles Rapshot 2024

The right of Charles Rapshot to be identified as the Author of
the Work has been asserted by him in accordance with the
Copyright, Designs and Patents Act 1988.

First published in 2024 by Headline Welbeck Non-Fiction[
An imprint of Headline Publishing Group

2

Apart from any use permitted under UK copyright law, this publication may
only be reproduced, stored, or transmitted, in any form, or by any means,
with prior permission in writing of the publishers or, in the case of
reprographic production, in accordance with the terms of licences
issued by the Copyright Licensing Agency.

Cataloguing in Publication Data is available from the British Library.

Hardback ISBN 978 1 0354 2548 8

Illustrations © Shutterstock.com

Typeset by EM&EN
Printed and bound in Great Britain by Clays Ltd, Elcograf S.p.A.

Headline's policy is to use papers that are natural, renewable and recyclable
products and made from wood grown in well-managed forests and other
controlled sources. The logging and manufacturing processes are expected
to conform to the environmental regulations of the country of origin.

HEADLINE PUBLISHING GROUP
An Hachette UK Company
Carmelite House
50 Victoria Embankment
London EC4Y 0DZ

The authorised representative in the EEA is Hachette Ireland, 8 Castlecourt
Centre, Dublin 15, D15 XTP3, Ireland (email: info@hbgi.ie)

www.headline.co.uk
www.hachette.co.uk

CONTENTS

Introduction — vii

The basic rules of golf — 1

Excuses to help you get out of the house and on to the course — 9

Excuses for when you really can't be arsed to get out of the house and on to the course — 23

Excuses for being bad at golf — 33

Golfing slang for bad shots — 45

A fool-proof guide to finding lost balls — 55

How to deal with divots	67
Inspirational quotes for bad golfers	77
Stories of other people's failures and the worst golfer of all time	97
Alternative game formats	109
Ways to be bad at golf and still enjoy it	121
What kind of bad golfer are you?	129
The 19th hole: a step-by-step guide	141
Conclusion: what have we learnt?	155
Acknowledgements	163

INTRODUCTION

It's a beautiful Sunday morning. You got up early, made yourself a coffee and crept out of the house without waking anyone. As you step on to the soft padding of the course, you stop and align your feet, taking in the incredible view in front of you. A series of immaculately maintained fairways open up before you, like green carpet stretched out into the misty distance.

As you close your eyes for a second and take in a big breath of crisp air, you realise you've managed to get up in time to catch the dawn chorus of birds outside. The silence is captivating, and reminds you why you get up so early. Life is quiet and simple . . . just you, the birds and the game you love: golf. It's at this moment that you remember that the world truly is wonderful.

You pull a pristine new Titleist Pro V1 (other balls are available) out of the front pocket, feeling its heft in your hand, and grab a tee from your pocket. You get a genuine shudder of excitement, a thrilling buzz up your body, as you pick the driver out of your bag.

Placing your hands with precision and care on your club, you lean slightly over

and turn your head out to the horizon.
You take another deep breath, feeling
the cold air enter your lungs and, once
again, savour the beauty of the moment.

Shuffling into position, you begin your
carefully honed swing routine –
shoulder turn, wrists bowed, in-to-out
swing. Your full energy transfers through
the grip, down the stiff-flex shaft into
the carbon face of the driver, into what
feels like the cleanest hit of your life . . .

'Fore!' shouts someone from behind you.

And, as your ball speeds towards the
starter's head, sending him diving for
cover, you remember that you actually

hate this stupid game . . . meanwhile that pristine Pro V1 is lost, forty-five degrees off target, in the next post-code. 'Mulligan?'

We've all been there, don't worry. Golf is life, but life is also pain, so, ergo, golf is pain. All the best golfers know it, as do the worst ones.

But fear not, this book is here to dull the pain, to make light of the darkness and to stop your long walk being *completely* ruined.

The Golfer's Survival Guide is full of fun tips, tricks and games to help you suck less at golf, or at least if you do still suck, to have a little bit more fun doing it.

I hope it'll help you realise that you're not alone (yep, there's been a long line of similarly crap golfers before you), to enjoy what is supposed to be a 'fun' activity and to survive the sinking feeling of hitting your fourth bunker of the day. And if it doesn't, at least you can tear it to pieces in frustration.

The basic rules of golf

(you know, just in case)

Sometimes it's good to go back to the basics. And sometimes, it's best to just start from the very beginning. So here's an idiot's guide . . .

- Golf is a sport

- It is mostly played by some humans, but occasionally by small animals (according to YouTube)

- You play by hitting a ball across a course using what is called a club

- Golf tends to be played in a round of eighteen holes (although nine's fine if you've got some place to be)

- Each hole has a teeing-off area, which marks the beginning of the hole

- Each hole also has a putting green, an area of shorter-cropped grass, in which you'll find a literal hole

- The hole is demarcated by a flag placed in the hole (as otherwise it would be quite hard to see)

- The aim of the game is to hit the ball from the teeing area and, using a number of strokes, get it into the hole

- A player plays with only one ball per hole (more when you lose your first ... which you will)

- Wherever the ball lands, the player hits from next (unless the ball is under water, has entered an area marked Out of Bounds or ends up in a crocodile's mouth)

- If we exclude the fancier golf scoring systems, the number of strokes it takes a player to get the ball into the literal hole becomes that player's score for that hole

- The cumulative score across the eighteen holes is your score for the game

- The player with the lowest cumulative score at the end of the eighteen holes wins

- All players must go home either miserable or elated. Don't let me catch you feeling OK.

Excuses to help you get out of the house and on to the course

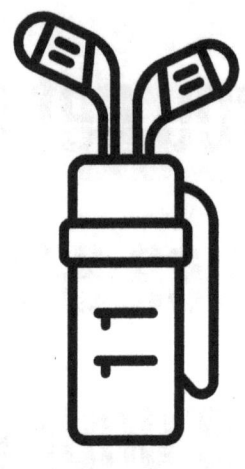

OK, now you've grasped the basics, let's move on to the next very important step of playing golf . . . actually making sure you get out of the house.

Like all addictions, golf is really quite bad for you. It takes up large swathes of your time, keeps you from having meaningful relationships with your loved ones and ultimately leaves you unsatisfied and wanting more . . . which is exactly why you have to make sure you keep going back regularly and topping yourself up.

To help you do so, here are some ready-made excuses, for any situation you find yourself in and anyone you find yourself having to escape from. Use liberally.

EXCUSES FOR YOUR BOSS

'I'm working from home tomorrow'
(this works particularly well when coupled with a 'can't believe I have to be inside when it's going to be such a glorious day outside')

(in response to 'What are you doing tomorrow?')
'God, what am I not doing tomorrow?'

'I do love Budget Stuff, but I really wish it didn't take up my whole Friday'

'I have jury duty'

(a great one, as it gives you a minimum of two weeks off)

'I'm ill'

(and then cough)

'My child is ill'

(and then get your child to cough)

'I'm writing a book . . . About what? . . . about, errr . . . golf'

'I'm doing that volunteering thing.
Yep, love those starving . . . kids'

'I'll be out meeting Jimmy Fontaine
from WBMGA'
*(or similarly important-sounding made-up
name and corporate abbreviation)*

EXCUSES FOR YOUR PARTNER

'I forgot to tell you, I went to the doctor and he said I needed to be outside for at least four hours every Saturday and/or Sunday morning'

'I'm going for a walk'

'The dog needs a walk'
(difficult one to pull off without taking the dog with you)

'The cat needs a walk'
(foolproof . . . cats don't need walks)

'I said I'd meet my friends for a thing'
(recommend including some details, but not too many)

'The club is having an emergency membership meeting'

'My new set of golf clubs needs knocking in'

'I need to return my friend's driver'

'My clubs will rust without regular usage'

'I think I left my favourite club-head cover at the back of the 1st tee'

'I forgot to rake the bunker'

'They need some help with the 19th hole'

'I'm popping to the shops . . . be back in four or five hours'

'I need to go out. I can't tell you why, but I can tell you it's someone special's birthday coming up.'
(needs to be within reasonable distance from your partner's birthday, and does need to be backed up with a decent present on said birthday, but this one can be used for months)

'I'm doing that volunteering thing. Yep, love those starving . . . animals'

'I'm having an affair'
(can only be used once, or twice max.)

'Golf is the love of my life'
(similar repercussions to the affair one)

EXCUSES FOR YOUR CHILDREN

'When you're old enough, you'll understand'

'Because I'm a grown-up and grown-ups make the decisions'

'Look, what's that over there?!'
(and then run out quickly)

Excuses for when you really can't be arsed to get out of the house and on to the course

Obviously, the entire premise of the previous section (and, indeed, of this book) is that you do actually want to go play golf, but if you're really sick of spending your weekends/some weekdays either getting your arse kicked or, let's be honest, kicking your own arse, then here is a set of excuses for fellow players.

Some of them may fight you, chase you on the phone, send you numerous texts asking why you don't want to come, but ultimately, remember, they play this awful game too, so they get it (and are probably wondering if they, too, should just sack it off and enjoy their day instead).

And if they really are insistent about giving you a hard time about it, just make a mental note to throw their ball in the bushes next time you get the chance.

Anyway, to the (entirely realistic) excuses . . .

'I have smallpox'
(cough)

'My kid has smallpox'
(get kid to cough)

'I've got to take the dog for a walk. It's been weeks. The vet's very angry at me.'

'I've got to take the cat for a walk.'
(again . . . genius)

'Looks like tornado weather'
(particularly hard one to pull off outside of the Southern states of the US)

'I saw this documentary about long walks and fresh air being really bad for you'

'Not after the way that squirrel looked at me last time. What if it's there again?!'

'I'm really into this puzzle'
(nothing to be ashamed of)

'Spending some time with the kids. One of them asked who I was the other day'

'Tired'

'Hungover'

'Wondering what it's all about'

'Broke all clubs in a fit of rage after last game'
(people will believe you)

'The dog ate my golf balls'

'I'll play when I'm better at the game'

'I'd actually just prefer not to'

'Can't, sorry, busy'

'Because it sucks'

'What's the point? The world is a cruel and empty place, devoid of meaning, created by and perpetuated by randomness. The universe is already so full of pain and suffering, seemingly without much point, so why would I spend my Saturday playing and very rarely being good at a game that, in the grand scheme of things, means nothing? And that's without even going into whether or not we're living in a simulation, which we almost certainly are. Just . . . why?'

Excuses for being bad at golf

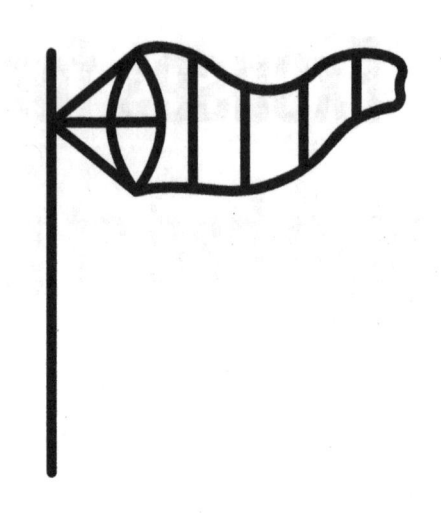

Obviously, you can't get out of every game. You've made this sport way too much of your identity to back out now and you have friends there . . . I guess.

So, for the days when you couldn't get out of it, and find yourself on the course, seemingly magnetically drawn to hitting your ball into the car park, here are some excuses . . . you know, for when you need them (which, let's be brutally honest, you always do).

EXCUSES DURING THE ROUND

'Too much wind'

'Not enough wind'

'Sun was in my eyes'

'Told you hitting it with the outside of your foot doesn't work'

'Mentally already in the pub'

'Forgot the rules' (see page 13)

'Dropping behind for a more dramatic victory'

'I needed to go get something from my car anyway'

'I'd actually rather *not* go to the pub'

'Getting those out of the way early'

'Feels like rain'

'Oh, yeah, I was aiming for the 15th.
Are we not on that hole?'

'Might have put too much gas on that one'

'The contact was too good'
(one for the bunker)

'It's the wrong type of sand'
(another bunker classic)

'Ah – they must not have updated the yardages since moving the hole'

'I've got the shanks today'

'Pitch mark made it bobble'

'Terrible lie'

'What's that over there?!'
(and then run away quickly)

'Goal!'

'I can't really hit right unless everyone within twenty feet of me is singing Taylor Swift's classic 'Shake It Off'. Would you mind?'

EXCUSES POST-ROUND

'Forgot my glove'

'Forgot my lucky glove . . . this is an unlucky one'

'Forgot my balls, and I can only play with Maxfli Red Dot specials. No, they still make them . . . I think'

'My back was playing up'

'Had a twinge in my neck'

'I could really feel my kidneys today'

'Must have eaten something bad'

'I was carrying a lot of pain in my lower feet'

'Work issues'

'Work stress'

'Getting cancelled right now'

'Didn't get enough sleep'

'Got too much sleep'

'My life hurts'

'Existential angst'

'I'm lost in a sea of ennui'

'You gotta laugh'

(and then promptly cry)

'I'm just doing this for the story'

'My head wasn't really in the game. Do you ever wonder what *Inception* was all about?'

'Everyone makes mistakes. Mine was coming here today'

Golfing slang for bad shots

(to help make light of that terrible putt)

OK, so you've tried making excuses, but a bad shot is still a bad shot. Now you've accepted that it's all gone horribly wrong, try making light of the situation by working out what *kind* of bad shot you just masterfully hit.

Thankfully, the golfing world has already named (and shamed) your bad shots, so here is a list. Try and work out where yours lands . . .

- **The Arthur Scargill** – good strike, poor result

- **The Saddam Hussein** – going from bunker to bunker

- **The Umberto Eco** – a putt that's impossible to read

- **The Nigel Farage** – a shot that goes way right

- **The Jeremy Corbyn** – a shot that wings unashamedly left

- **The Bad Beckham** – a bendy one, but less on-target

- **The Christopher Columbus** – a shot that ends up far from where it was meant to

- **The Ferdinand Magellan** – a shot that, quite simply, gets lost

- **The Tarzan** – one that flies through the trees

- **The Michael Phelps** – a shot that loves the water

- **The Blockbuster** – a drive that goes high and falls sharply

- **The Icarus** – flies into the sun, never to be seen again

- **The Mr Jelly** – wobbles bloody everywhere

- **The Soggy Chip** – the chip-shot that no one wants

- **The Rocky** – a shot that just keeps skipping

- **The Flat Stanley** – a shot that's thinner than an After Eight mint

- **The Old Banger** – keeps putt-putting until it finally explodes

- **The Kelly Slater** – all air, no distance

- **The Hoverboard** – one of those drives that stays about six inches from the ground for its entire flight

- **The Steve Redgrave** – the water's its natural habitat

- **The Bear Grylls** – actively seeking the wilderness

- **The Soapbox Derby** – once it's on the road, nothing's stopping it

- **The Pinball Wizard** – bounces this way and that, keeping you guessing, but ultimately, it's game over

A fool-proof guide to finding lost balls

Are you single-handedly keeping the golf ball industry afloat with your errant drives? Perhaps your lake-bound bounces are contributing to rising water levels at your local course? Or you're worried that you've replaced your Titleists with active camouflage balls?

Well, you're not alone, and us bad golfers have to stick together. That's why this section will include not only fool-proof tips but also a handy step-by-confused-step guide to help you find your lost balls. Hope it helps.

STEP 1: So, despite your best efforts (and your promise to yourself never to do it again), you've just hit a wildly terrible ball (see variations in previous section). You are, naturally, overcome with a powerful urge to close your eyes, scream at the sky, curse the gods that brought you to this godforsaken place in your life and, opening your eyes for just a second to check you're not going to seriously injure a fellow player (but in total disregard for the lovely turf you've just hit from), plough your club into the ground, over and over again, until both the turf and your club are shadows of their former selves.

But here's an idea . . . instead of doing *that* (much as it is incredibly satisfying and incredibly likely to get you banned from yet another course), why don't you try looking where your shot goes? Just an idea. Don't look at me like that. Put the club down.

STEP 2: Once you've seen roughly where it's gone, pick a landmark as close as possible to where it went. This could be a big rock, a particularly dented tree or that hole you made in the ground last time you were here. Remember that landmark, and maybe even tell someone near you where you're headed for, just in case you forget on the long walk to the spot (it went pretty far).

STEP 3: Walk, as quickly as possible, to that landmark in as straight a line as possible. If you get lost on the way to your lost ball, we can't help you. Take it as an indication that you truly are beyond salvation and just start again. Or pick a different sport. Both good ideas.

STEP 4: When you get to the landmark, place a tee in the ground in front of it. This is in case, after entering the dense line of trees, or braving it into the thick bushes, or wading into the lake, you lose track of where you started. You literally only have that landmark, so don't bloody lose it.

STEP 5: Notice the exact point of entry the ball made into the trees/bushes/lake/cafeteria and, using the following calculation, work out the exact place it will have landed after it disappeared from view.

$$\frac{\text{Power of hit (kJ)} \times \text{angle of release} / \text{wind speed velocity (km/h)}}{\text{Density of foliage (branches/sqm)} + \text{softness of ground (10 = jelly} - \text{1 = tight)}}$$

(Just joking, we know you're not clever enough to do this . . . you are, after all, spending your Saturday sweatily looking for a lost golf ball.)

STEP 6: Once you get into the area of interest, take a deep breath and soften your gaze. Try not to look at any one thing in particular, but just survey your surroundings with soft eyes. Your golf ball was made in that colour to stand out against the natural surroundings, so really it should be easy to find. I mean, what natural feature is white . . . apart from stones . . . and what kind of sick bastard puts white stones in a place you're looking for a golf ball?!

STEP 7: If this doesn't work, you just have to start moving things. It's OK, the people who own the course know this is the case. So, whether it's picking up white stones and throwing them as far as you can or taking out your broken, bent club and hacking away at long-grass, crush your natural environment and teach it a lesson for hiding your ball from you.

STEP 8: If, after all this, you still can't find your ball, just give up. Buy some of those fancy balls you can track with an app. You deserve it.

How to deal with divots

According to George Waters at the USGA (United States Golf Association), 'taking divots is a normal part of any round of golf'. I've seen a video online of Rory McIlroy taking a divot, and it's described as 'mesmerising'. But there's taking a divot . . . and then there's sending a chunk of earth to another postcode.

But sometimes (OK, all the time) you can't help it, so here are some handy tips for when you just need to replace, fill or run away from a divot.

REPLACING A DIVOT

o Check your divot and see if there is still grass attached

o Place it back in the ground (in the correct orientation – you have to cover those tracks)

o Use your foot to press down on the divot. Using your foot is the best technique, as it matches the pressure the surface is prepared for (and that other players will be used to), so stops additional wells developing.

- Even out the edges as much as possible and as lovingly as possible using the heel of your foot at first, graduating to the toe area for fine adjustment.

- Act really pleased with yourself, so that any onlookers believe you've actually done a good job.

FILLING A DIVOT

Sometimes the wild swing was just a little too wild (we've all been there . . . just not quite as much as you . . . maybe calm it down a little) and there is no grass attached or the turf in question is a shadow of its former self. If this is the case, what do you do?

- At very fancy courses, 'divot filler' might be a thing – a sandy mixture in a bottle-like device in the tee area. If so, apply, smooth the mixture out and press down with your foot.

- In the ninety-nine times out of one hundred there isn't divot filler, make a token effort to look like you're atoning for your crime by searching around for a divot that hasn't been returned. If you do find one, bingo! Replace as advised above.

- Put down this book and again, look very happy with yourself. Maybe you could brush your hands off, in suggestion of a brilliant job well done, or even say to yourself (though as loudly as it takes for someone else to hear) 'Brilliant job well done'.

Now that you know how it's done, go wild! Actually, sorry, not too wild. That's how you got into this mess in the first place. Look . . . just try not to get kicked off the course this time.

Inspirational quotes for bad golfers

In the hope they inspire you to suck less . . .

(one of these has to work)

'I have a tip that can take five strokes off anyone's game: it is called an eraser.'
Arnold Palmer

'I know I am getting better at golf because I am hitting fewer spectators.'
Gerald Ford

'A great shot is when you pull it off. A smart shot is when you don't have the guts to try it.'
Phil Mickelson

'Golf is a game in which you yell fore, shoot six and write down five.'
Paul Harvey, American radio broadcaster

'Golf: a plague invented by the Calvinistic Scots as a punishment for man's sins.'
James Barrett Reston, American journalist

'The woods are full of long drivers.'
Harvey Penick, American pro golfer, coach and writer

'Forget the last shot. It takes so long to accept that you can't always replicate your swing. The only thing you can control is your attitude toward the next shot.'
Mark McCumber

'I don't let birdies and pars get in the way of having a good time.'
Angelo Spagnolo, author

'I'm the best, I just haven't played yet.'
Muhammad Ali

'Mistakes are part of the game. It's how well you recover from them, that's the mark of a great player.'
Alice Cooper

'You know what they say about big hitters . . . the woods are full of them.'
Jimmy Demaret, first three-time winner of the Masters

'Golf is a compromise between what your ego wants you to do, what experience tells you to do and what your nerves let you do.'
Bruce Crampton, former Australian golfer

'Golf is assuredly a mystifying game. It would seem that if a person has hit a golf ball correctly a thousand times, he could be able to duplicate the performance at will. But such is certainly not the case.'
Bobby Jones, multiple major winner and co-founder of the Masters

'A perfectly straight shot with a big club is a fluke.'
Jack Nicklaus

'Forget your opponents: always play against par.'
Sam Snead

'Golf is about how well you accept, respond to and score with your misses much more so than it is a game of your perfect shots.'
Dr Bob Rotella, author

'Never concede the putt that beats you.'
Harry Vardon

'You don't have the game you played last year or last week. You only have today's game. It may be far from your best, but that's all you've got. Harden your heart and make the best of it.'
Walter Hagen

'It took me seventeen years to get three thousand hits in baseball. It took one afternoon on the golf course.'
Hank Aaron, legendary baseball player

'The mind messes up more shots than the body.'
Tommy Bolt, US Open-winning American golfer

'Golf is a game you can never get too good at. You can improve, but you can never get to where you master the game.'
Gay Brewer, Masters-winning American golfer

'Discipline and concentration are a matter of being interested.'
Tom Kite, US Open-winning American golfer

'The most important shot in golf is the next one.'
Ben Hogan

'No matter how good you get, you can always get better – and that's the exciting part.'
Tiger Woods

'Every shot counts. The three-foot putt is as important as the 300-yard drive.'
Henry Cotton, English golfer and three-time winner of The Open

'The golf swing is like a suitcase into which we are trying to pack one too many things.'
John Updike

'It's how you deal with failure that determines how you achieve success.'
David Feherty, broadcaster and former pro player

'Golf . . . is the infallible test. The man who can go into a patch of rough alone, with the knowledge that only God is watching him, and play his ball where it lies, is the man who will serve you faithfully and well.'
P. G. Wodehouse

'Golf is played by twenty million mature American men whose wives think they are out having fun.'
Jim Bishop, author and journalist

'My swing is so bad, I look like a caveman killing his lunch.'
Lee Trevino

'Everybody can see that my swing is homegrown. That means everybody has a chance to do it.'
Bubba Watson

'The only time my prayers are never answered is on the golf course.'
Billy Graham, American evangelist

'You've got to have the guts not to be afraid to screw up.'
Fuzzy Zoeller

'Golf can best be defined as an endless series of tragedies obscured by the occasional miracle.'
Anonymous

'Golf is the hardest game in the world. There is no way you can ever get it. Just when you think you do, the game jumps up and puts you in your place.'
Ben Crenshaw

'They call it golf because all the other four letter words were taken.'
Raymond Floyd

'The value of routine: trusting your swing.'
Lorii Myers, entrepreneur and author

'If profanity had an influence on the flight of the ball, the game of golf would be played far better than it is.'
Horace G. Hutchinson, English amateur player of the late 19th and early 20th century

'The more I practice, the luckier I get.'
Gary Player

'Life is not fair, so why should I make a course that is fair?'
Pete Dye, American course designer

'Golf gives you an insight into human nature, your own as well as your opponent's.'
Grantland Rice, American sports writer of the early 20th century

'Happiness is a long walk with a putter.'
Greg Norman

'A bad attitude is worse than a bad swing.'
Payne Stewart

'There's going to be places where you can attack the golf course and there's going to be times where you've got to kind of bite your lip and play conservative and hit to certain spots on the green, get out of there with a par and move on.'

Jim Furyk

'If you watch a game, it's fun. If you play it, it's recreation. If you work at it, it's golf.'

Bob Hope

'Why am I using a new putter? Because the last one didn't float too well.'

Craig Stadler

'Golf is a fascinating game. I've taken nearly 40 years to discover that I can't play it.'
Ted Ray, English comedian of the 1940s, 50s and 60s

'Golf is a game whose aim is to hit a very small ball into an even smaller hole, with weapons singularly ill-designed for the purpose.'
Winston Churchill

Stories of other people's failures and the worst golfer of all time

(to make you feel a bit better)

OTHER PEOPLE'S FAILURES

In 2012, at The Open, Aussie prodigy Adam Scott was up by four shots with only four holes to play. Throughout his first decade as a professional, Scott had only four top-ten finishes in the Majors, and in 2009 he had even dropped out of the world's top fifty. But now, here he was, leading The Open by four shots from Ernie Els. But then Scott bogeyed the 15th. Then the 16th. His lead was down to two shots and Ernie Els was now on his heels. When Els holed a fifteen-foot putt on the 18th, the lead was one. Meanwhile, Scott was struggling on the 17th, picking up another bogey. And finally, on the 18th, he got one last bogey. Scott lost by one. Bet you wish someone would pay you to do that.

For most of his career, Ed Sneed was assumed to be the son or nephew of legendary player Sam Snead. Did they just think that Ed couldn't spell his own surname, I wonder? Sometimes, course officials even 'corrected' it to 'Snead' on their scoreboards! That was, until the 1979 Masters, when Ed was in a sudden-death playoff against Fuzzy Zoeller, who was playing his first ever Masters. And naturally for this section, Zoeller sunk an eight-foot putt for a birdie and Sneed bogeyed the last three holes to suffer one of the most infamous defeats in Masters history. No one would ever forget Ed's name again.

Probably the largest lead blown on our list . . . in the 1996 Masters, Greg Norman was five shots ahead of Nick Faldo at the end of the 5th hole. After three bogeys and two double-bogeys in the last ten holes, he finished his day on 78. Faldo won by five shots. The story that has emerged since is that Norman spoke with sports psychologist Rick Jensen. Norman was playing terribly going into the Masters and asked Jensen what he could do to get control of his ball. In a line that has gone down in history, Jenson asked Norman 'Really, how bad could you be hitting it?'

No discussion of golf's greatest collapses would be complete without mention of Jean Van de Velde. In the 1999 Open, van de Velde had a three-shot lead going into the 18th, but triple-bogeyed the hole and ultimately lost the Open in a playoff. While we all have tragic stories, very few of us will go down in golfing history, but that's probably because very few of us would, with a stony face, take our shoes and socks off and roll up our trouser legs in front of millions of people and wade into the water. But respect to van de Velde for doing it, and without batting an eyelid.

THE WORST GOLFER OF ALL TIME

According to his unpublished memoirs, shipyard-worker Maurice Flitcroft became a golfer because, as he recalls, 'I was looking to find fame and fortune, but only achieved one of the two.' He said he was inspired to enter The Open Championship by Walter Danecki, a postal worker from Milwaukee, who managed to enter the 1965 Open Championship after telling the R&A that he was a pro. Danecki shot a two-round score of 221.

Flitcroft tried the same approach: he told the R&A that he was a professional. Unfortunately, he was royally found out at the 1976 Open when he managed a score 121, which was 49 over par and has gone down as the worst score in the tournament's history. Some of the players he was partnered up with successfully demanded a refund of their fee, more than one yelled at him and following the '76 Open, the rules were changed to prevent Flitcroft from entering again.

Despite this, he would regularly attempt to enter The Open and other competitions, using false moustaches, dark glasses and a succession of fake names, including Gene Paychecki (as in 'pay cheque'),

Arnold Palmtree and Count Manfred von Hoffmanstel.

Flitcroft's fame led to numerous golf trophies being named after him, and the Blythe Country Club in Michigan even began the Maurice Gerald Flitcroft Member-Guest Tournament in 1978. By the 22nd year of the tournament, the club featured a green with two holes (so that many approaches would work) and one that had a twelve-inch cup.

In its obituary of Flitcroft, the *Daily Telegraph* said: 'Maurice Flitcroft . . . was a chain-smoking shipyard crane-operator from Barrow-in-Furness whose persistent attempts to gatecrash the British Open golf championship produced a sense-of-humour failure among members of the golfing establishment.' What a hero.

Alternative game formats

(for when the regular rules
just aren't working)

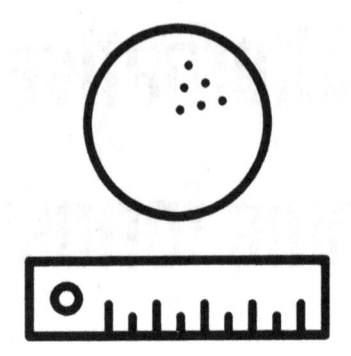

You've tried excusing yourself from the game, you've tried practising more, you've tried getting some wise words from the greats. But if none of that seems to be working, there is one brilliant way to change your fortunes . . . change the rules.

What do you mean 'you can't make up random rules to a sport that's been played for hundreds of years'?!
Just watch me.

Feel free to join in and make up your own too. Whatever helps you improve. Come on, we both need this win now.

- **The Upside Down** – <u>Most</u> strokes wins (Yeah, that's right).

- **The Lakehouse** – Closest to the lake without getting it in wins the hole.

- **The Swimmer** – Most balls in the lake wins the game.

- **Worst-ball Scramble** – When playing in pairs, you have to play the worst ball from the pair.

- **Reverse Mulligans** – Where you have to make the other player replay a shot when they've hit it well.

- **Ronaldo Rules** – In addition to your shot, you can also take one 'free kick', where you are allowed to kick your ball into a better location. You also get a stroke taken off your score (or one added, depending on whether you're playing the first Alternative Rule above) if you do the Ronaldo goal celebration after.

- **Birdies Buy Drinkies** – For every birdie your opponent gets, they buy you a drink (that should shut the smug bastards up).

- **Shank Bingo** – At any time during an opponent's swing, a player can shout 'Shank!' really loudly and if the opponent shanks their shot because of the loud and obnoxious distraction, the player who shouted gets an extra point.

- **Ridiculous Relay** – Players decide a set order-of-play (Player 1, Player 2, Player 3 etc.). After each ball, the next ball the player will play will be the number above them in the order (so Player 2 plays Player 1's ball, Player 3 plays Player 2's ball and Player 1 goes to the bottom of the pile, etc.). At the next ball, it moves in the same direction again, so that you never play the same ball twice. (The nature of this game and the fact that no one ever plays their opponent's ball well has been known to anger anyone else on the course, so avoid this when there are other people waiting).

- **Double or Quits** – After striking their first ball, but before their ball lands, each player has the opportunity to shout either 'Double' or 'Quits'. 'Double' doubles the score of that hole, 'Quits' negates it. Each player can use each one once in a round.

- **El Capitan** – Based on the popular card game, at the end of a hole, the person who did best becomes El Capitan and gets to make up one rule that applies for the remainder of the round.

- **Wildcard Baby!** – In a round of golf, each player has one wildcard, where they can take their ball and swap it for any other player's on that same hole. So your terrible shot into the trees can suddenly become that wonderful chip on to the green that your mate just played. One warning, though . . . if you don't shout the full phrase 'Wildcard Baby!', it doesn't count and you lose your wildcard altogether.

- **Monopoly** – All players leave the course and just play a game of Monopoly. It's marginally more fun than golf and, even though it is a game of chance, you're probably still much better at it, so why not just have fun for once in your life?

Ways to be bad at golf and still enjoy it

OK, so I think we've tried just about everything now to make you into a good golfer (even changing the rules). I think we all (and by 'we' I mean you, and by 'all' I still mean you) just need to accept that we all are bad at golf. And with acceptance, hopefully, comes freedom. We can be bad at golf and still enjoy it.

However, if that sounds like a cop-out (which it definitely is), then here are some fun ideas for ways to be bad at golf and still enjoy it.

- Imagine an old-school sitcom-style laughter track behind every shot you take. Then, at least, you know the audience are enjoying it.

- Rank your worst shots, in order from terrible to embarrassing.

- Get drunk before the game (this does admittedly undermine page 153 a little, but hey, it's fun).

- Sing the entire *Hamilton* soundtrack, start to finish. Great musical.

- Narrate your entire game like a commentator watching the Masters. Go into your history, talk about your chequered record on this course, assess your stats, make predictions about whether today can be any different for you, try not to swear too much, comment on the unfortunate hat that woman is wearing, make a little joke about the controversy surrounding certain parts of your personal life outside of the game and whether the papers are just making up all the depraved antics, ask your fellow commentator if they feel like you really should have stuck to tennis – whatever it takes to get you through another god-awful day.

- Play Strip Golf, so every time you lose a hole to another player, you have to take an item of clothing off. You should probably wear some layers.

- Jog between balls. At least then you'd be getting some exercise. And visiting different corners of the car park.

- Try and name at least five things that is good about your game. That should take you a few hours and might distract you enough to actually become good.

- Become the flag girl for a Fast-and-Furious-style golf-cart drag race. Yes, I know it has nothing to do with golf, but still, life is hard enough as it is. Let's just do this for us.

- Start watching something on your phone. Who cares anyway?

What kind of bad golfer are you?

(find your people)

This section will offer a breakdown of the various types of bad golfer. That way, you can pinpoint exactly what's wrong with you (probably many things) and hopefully find some comfort in the fact that there are others like you (though no one quite as bad).

- **The Unlucky** – They could be good . . . they could be great . . . they could have been a contender! . . . if only their luck wasn't so so bad.

- **The Perfectionist** – Their gloves are crisp, their trousers are pressed, their feet just need shuffling a bit this way, their ideal conditions are not this windy. One day, everything will be perfect, but until then . . . they suck.

- **The Sandworm** – Like the sandworms from *Dune*, they seem to live in the sand. Every now and again, they emerge triumphantly, but outside of that, the bunker is their home.

- **The Looks** – Immaculately turned out, but all show. Also not very clever.

- **The Brains** – Knows the game inside-and-out. Has all the facts, all the knowledge, all the insight, none of the skill.

- **The Muscle** – All power. Constantly overshoots. Never learns their lesson.

- **The Wildcard** – You never know what's going to happen with them. You could guess (it's mostly terrible), but they can always surprise you.

- **The Techy** – Always has the latest gadgets, apps and tech. Doesn't do them much good.

- **The Filler** – You only really invited them to make up the numbers. It's OK, we all do it. Just don't tell them that their main value is being free when no one else was.

- **The Ticking Suitcase** – That's right, there's a bomb in there. A big one, like in the movies. Unlike the ones in the movies, though, this one doesn't have a timer on it . . . you have no idea when it's going to explode.

- **The Excavator** – Just loves digging into the ground. Can't get enough of it.

- **The Shanker** – Pretty self-explanatory. Just make sure they don't mishear you when you call them this. Although, actually, both are pretty bad.

- **The Forager** – Just loves getting into the bushes and searching around. Although foragers tend to find what they're looking for . . .

- **The Mathematician** – Really good at calculating scores, angles and distances. Just does badly at all of them.

- **The Sulker** – Will not forget the bad shot they played and will mope around constantly afterwards. It was nine holes ago, Brian, just let it go!

- **The Green-Eyed Monster** – Not the best category to fall into (maybe you could throw it on to someone else): they just can't keep it together when other players are on the green. Cursing their opponents' luck and celebrating their bad putts, this is not a good look.

- **The Unsatisfied** – Never enjoys their game, even when they're winning.

- **The Chauffeur** – Is only really here to drive the golf cart. In fairness to them, it is cool.

- **The Stuntman** – A sub-species of The Chauffeur. Despite knowing that golf carts only go at a maximum 10mph, they still do everything they can to catch some air, Tokyo Drift or roll the whole thing over in a blaze of glory and twisted plastic. Anything to distract from their game.

- **The Fun Bobby** – Brings the fun (and the wine). Neither of which help with their golf. Or mine, stupid Fun Bobby.

- **The Choker** – They are almost there. Just one more putt. It couldn't be easier. This is when The Choker really comes into their own and . . . well . . . chokes.

The 19th hole: a step-by-step guide

(finally, somewhere you can win)

Congratulations, you made it. Well, if you can call what just happened out there on the course 'making it'. No one died and you survived . . . and isn't that all anyone can really ask of you (particularly those who've seen you play golf before)? But also, that air shot on the second didn't put your back out, that shank on the seventh didn't catch anyone in any sensitive areas, no bones were fractured when you tried to break your very hard club over your very soft leg . . . basically, you got away with nothing but a damaged ego (and what you hope turns out to just be a massive bruise on your right thigh).

Now, though, it's finally your time to shine. You may have been hacking dents in golf courses for years, but you've been punching holes in your liver for *decades*. Not that you need it (you're going to absolutely *crush* this, I can feel it), but here is a step-by-step guide to really finishing on a high, to finally getting into your rhythm, to smashing arguably the most important hole of all . . . the 19th.

You got this.

STEP 1: Three-putt the 18th as per. Breathe a sigh of relief. Reassure yourself and your nervous system with the knowledge that it's over (well, for today, and anything beyond that is a problem for Future You).

STEP 2: Punch the air, so that people who are far away and who don't know you very well will think you just finished a momentous round. Little do they know, the fools.

STEP 3: Wipe the mixture of mud, sand, wildflowers and turf, all held together by sludgy lake water, off your clubs and strut off the green, like you meant everything that just happened over the past few hours.

STEP 4: As you walk towards the clubhouse, offer your fellow players some much-needed advice on their game. Some choice phrases could include 'you looked tense out there today, maybe try relaxing more', 'I feel like you should go back to the old swing' and 'I find that golf really is about your mindset . . . I have some techniques to help improve your mood on bad days, which I'll share later'. They love this.

STEP 5: Push open both doors to the clubhouse bar dramatically and exclaim 'another round like that and the club pro's going to out of a job' loudly enough for everyone to know for certain that you must be a brilliant golfer.

STEP 6: Walk up to the bar and if you won, buy the first round, and if you didn't win, (because I know it's been a while since that happened to you) allow the victor to buy the first round, but exclaim loudly 'OK, seeing as I'm *always* the first one buying drinks', so that everyone knows how great you are.

STEP 7: Finish that drink quickly.

STEP 8: Buy another drink, and finish that.

STEP 9: And another.

STEP 10: And another. Maybe a stronger one this time. Whatever it takes to forget what just happened.

STEP 11: Gather everyone round to hear tales of how you became such a master.

STEP 12: Challenge that big guy to an arm wrestle.

STEP 13: Challenge that guy who's always in here to a darts competition (though obviously now you need to use your other hand, because of the arm wrestle).

STEP 14: Do whatever it takes to *finally* win something. To *feel* something.

STEP 15: Have another drink. Oh, that's not yours. Never mind.

STEP 16: Get an Uber home. Ask the driver if he can play 'We Are The Champions' to cheer you up.

STEP 17: Get home and realise 'We Are The Champions' just made you even more sad.

STEP 18: Cry yourself to sleep.

STEP 19: Wake up and promise yourself you will neither drink nor play that awful game ever again.

STEP 20: Go back to the club (you need to pick up your car, after all), check you haven't been banned from ever returning again and if not, book in a tee time for next Saturday.

Conclusion: what have we learnt?

Let's see what you've actually learnt.
Probably nothing (you're not great
at things), but still, no harm in trying
(unless the club slips out of your hand
like it did last time) . . .

We learnt the basics. Always a good place to start.

We learnt excuses to help you get back on to the course.

We learnt excuses to stop you making the terrible decision to get back on to the course.

We learnt excuses for being terrible at golf.

We learnt entertaining names for the awful shots you play.

We learnt how to find lost balls.

We learnt how to deal with divots.

We heard from inspirational people that will hopefully inspire you to suck less.

We heard stories of other people's failures (and even about the worst golfer of all time . . . thankfully, not you).

We discovered alternative game formats (for when the original really isn't working for you).

We discovered ways to make having a terrible time at what should be an enjoyable game more manageable.

We explored all the different kinds of bad golfers (so you can help find your people).

We looked at how to end on a high (and by high, I mean somehow making your fellow players respect you even less than they already did ... which is some achievement).

So even if we didn't improve your game (it's just a book, not a divine miracle), I hope that together we have worked out a way for you to be bad at golf and still enjoy it. Because, let's be honest, you really need the win.